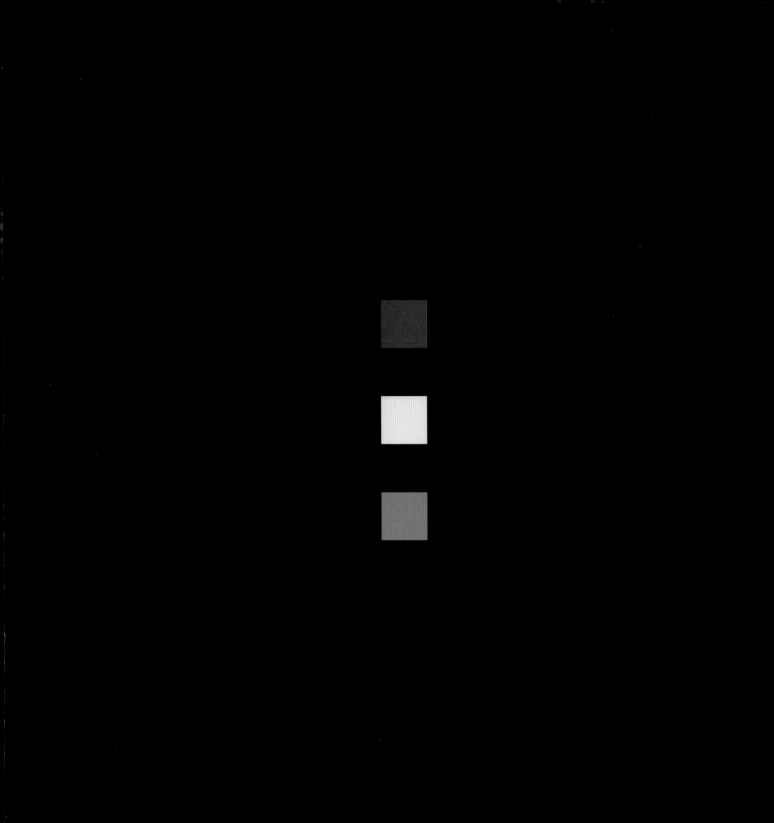

A World of Colors

Seeing Colors in a New Way

Marie Houblon

NATIONAL
GEOGRAPHIC

WASHINGTON, D.C.

Take a look at this
yellow sunflower.

Now see if you can find other yellow things.
Do you see...
A field of yellow wildflowers?
Yellow leather being cut?
Yellow umbrellas?
A yellow house with yellow shutters?

**Now take your eyes from the
book and look around you. Can you
find yellow in your world?**

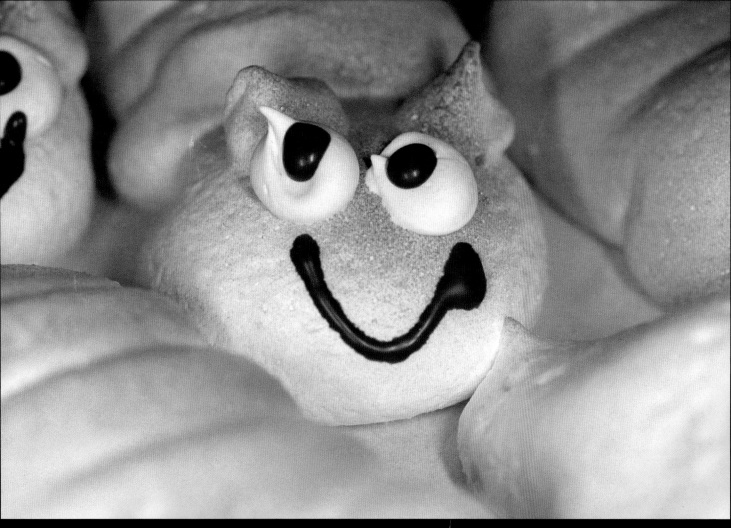

Check out the blue powdered sugar
on these friendly marshmallows.

Each color is really lots of different colors.
Do you see…
Blue doors?
A blue walkway?
A blue patterned skirt?
The blue light of evening?
Blue water?
Blue feet on a blue-footed booby?

Now look up. Do you see different blues in your world?

Green

Sometimes color can surprise you.
Did you think all bananas were yellow?
Think again.

Where do you see green in the pictures?
Can you find green moss on steps?
Green algae on green water?
Green trees on the side of a road?
A big green leaf being used as a raincoat?

Look around.
Can you find green in your world?

Color can camouflage. These boys' red jackets almost make them disappear against the red wall.

Color can make things stand out.
What red thing stands out in this picture?

And why is everything red in this dark circus
tent? Light can have color, too.

Find some red in your world.

Orange

Doesn't the color orange make

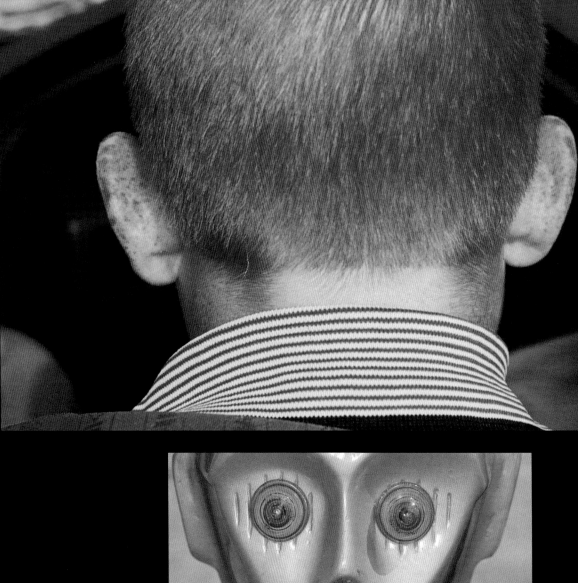

Orange usually stands out.
Find...
Orange eyes,
Orange tangerines, and
Orange hair
(Isn't it funny we call it "red"?)

Look around you to find orange.

Here's another funny color name.
These pink fish are called red snapper.

There's plenty of pink to find in these pictures:
Pink walls,
A pink apron,
A pink pig,
Pink plastic swans, and
A pink car.

**Go for a scavenger hunt to find
the pink in your world.**

Purple

Purple padded doors make this entryway look special.

Purple is special in these pictures, too.
Do you see...
Purple cloth flowers on a pretty hat?
Purple paint from a special celebration?

**Look for the special purple
in your world.**

Brown

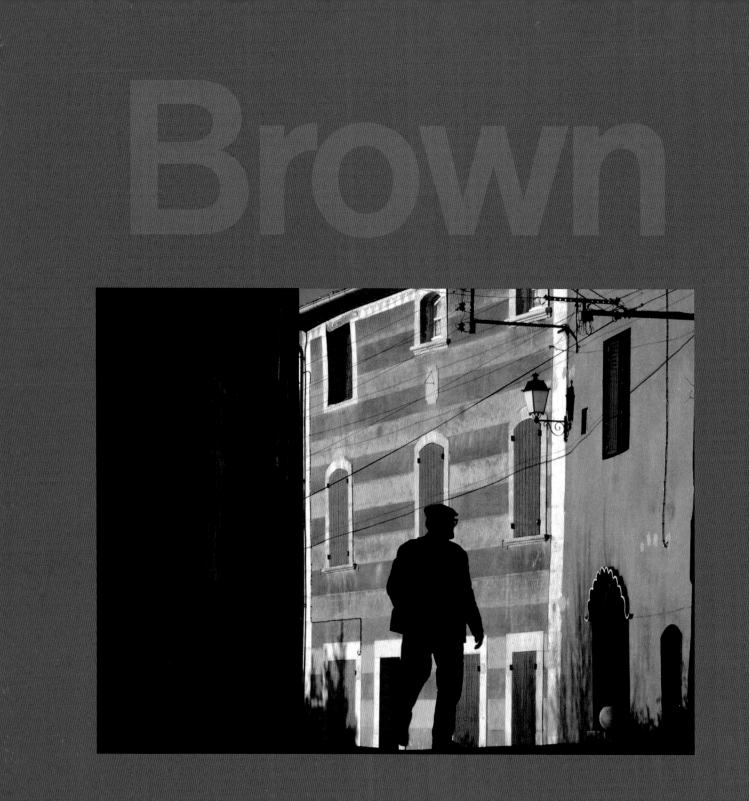

Brown stripes,
Brown shutters,
A solid brown wall, and
Brown doors.

Brown is the color of earth.
In this picture the rocks, the dirt, and
even the horse are brown.

I bet there's lots of brown in your world.

All colors mixed together make black,
and everything turns black without light.
Do you see...
Black birds?
The sun black in a black sky during
a daytime eclipse?

Where do you see black around you?

There's lots of gray in cities.
Find..
A gray-haired man in a gray hat and suit,
A gray building,
A gray winter tree, and a gray parking lot.

Look for the gray in your world.

White

White is no color at all.
Find...
White sheets and
A white snow angel in white snow.

Find the white in your world.

Colors are

What colors can you find
in these pictures?

everywhere

What colors can you find in your world?

Originally published in France by TOURBILLON S.A.S. under the title De quelles couleur © Tourbillon, 2004

English text copyright © 2009 National Geographic

English composite copyright © 2009 Tourbillon

Editorial and artistic concept development :
Franck Girard, Marie-Odile Fordacq and Marie Houblon

Photo editor :
Marie Houblon

French edition art direction :
Delphine Renon

English text :
Nancy Feresten

English edition art direction :
David M. Seager

Additional photo research :
Lori Epstein

Credits :
All photographs are from the archives of the Magnum Photo Agency and appear by permission of Magnum.
Cover: Gueorgui Pinkhassov—Paris, France—1999; p. 7: Dennis Stock—Provence, France—1980; p. 9 top left: Dennis Stock—Provence, France—1980; p. 9 top right: Bruno Barbey—Fez, Morocco—1984; p. 9 bottom left: Thomas Hoepker—Kyoto, Japan—1977; p. 9 bottom right: Miguel Rio Branco—Havana, Cuba—1994; p. 11: Martin Parr—Wellington, New Zealand—1998; p. 12 top: Alex Webb—Anse-a-Galets, Haiti—1986; p. 12 bottom left: Dennis Stock—Hawaii, USA—1980; p. 12 bottom right: Stuart Franklin—Galapagos Islands, Equador—1997; p. 15: David Alan Harvey—Costa Rica—2001; p. 16 :

Ferdinando Scianna—Benares, India—1997; p. 17: Steve McCurry—Nepal—1983; p. 19 Gueorgui Pinkhassov— Paris, France—1999; p. 20 Miguel Rio Branco—Madrid, Spain—1995; p. 21: Miguel Rio Branco—Rio de Janeiro, Brazil—1993; p. 23: Martin Parr—Wales, United Kingdom—1995; p. 24 top: Martin Parr—Ireland—1997; p. 24 bottom: Martin Parr—United Kingdom—1998; p. 25: Richard Kalvar—Japan—19983; p. 27: Miquel Rio Branco—Brazil—1990; p. 28: David Alan Harvey—Oaxaca, Mexico—1992; p. 29 top: Chris Steele-Perkins—Mount Fuji, Japan—2001; p. 29 bottom: Ian Berry—Berlin, Germany—2000; p. 31—Peter Marlow—London, United Kingdom—2001; p. 32 top: Martin Parr—London, United Kingdom—2000;

p. 32 bottom : David Alan Harvey—Trinidad and Tobago—1993; p. 35: Thomas Hoepker—Arizona, USA—1995; p. 39: Bruno Barbey—Essaouira, Morroco—1997; p. 37: Dennis Stock—Provence, France—1980; p. 38 Bruno Barbey—Mauritius—1992; p. 39: Philip Jones Griffiths—Cambodia—1995; p. 40: Peter Marlow—Saluzzo, Italy—2003; p. 41: Lise Sarfati—Dreux, France—1998; p. 42: Peter Marlow—Argentiere, France—2001; p. 43: Peter Marlow—United Kingdom—2002; p. 44: Martin Parr—United Kingdom—2000; p. 45: Ferdinando Scianna—Mexico City, Mexico—1988.

Library of Congress Cataloging-in-Publication Data available upon request
Trade hardcover
ISBN: 978-1-4263-0556-6
Library edition
ISBN:978-1-4263-0559-7

For more information, please call 1-800-NGS LINE (647-5463) or write to the following address:

National Geographic Society 1145 17th Street N.W., Washington, D.C. 20036-4688 U.S.A.

Visit us online at www.nationalgeographic.com/books

For librarians and teachers: www.ngchildrensbooks.org

More for kids from National Geographic: kids.nationalgeographic.com

For information about special discounts for bulk purchases, please contact National Geographic Books Special Sales: ngspecsales@ngs.org

For rights or permissions inquiries, please contact National Geographic Books Subsidiary Rights: ngbookrights@ngs.org

Printed in China

09/SNP/1

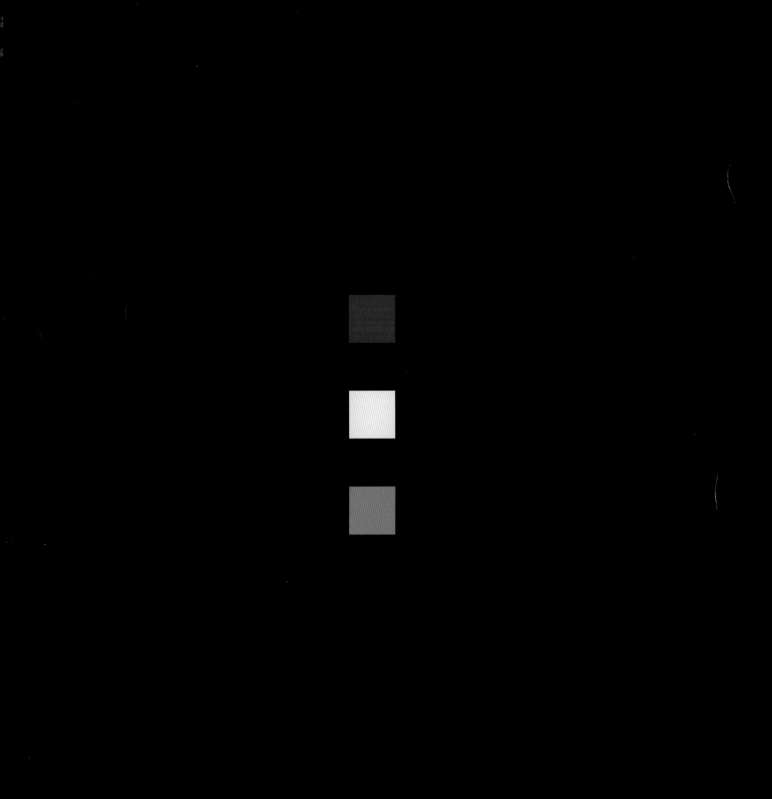